"O ALLAH! YOU ARE MY DESTINATION,
AND YOUR PLEASURE IS MY PURPOSE"

DIVINE SALAWAT AND BLESSINGS BE UPON OUR MASTER
(SAYYIDUNA) MUHAMMAD, MESSENGER OF ALLAH, AND
UPON HIS NOBLE HOUSEHOLD (AHLUL BAYT)

Published by the author: Sayyid Dr Sharif Sayid Alhusaini, 2019 (1440 AH), Naqshalanwar Publications, UK

Book Title: 'Prayers of the Muslim Saints: Naqshabandi Supplications'

ISBN: 978-0-995665644

All designs by: Alsharif Naqshalanwar Designers ©

Printed in the United Kingdom

For more knowledge on the Blessed Naqshabandi Madani Tariqa, please see blog: puresunnah.blogspot.com

ACKNOWLEDGEMENT

May Allah reward my Master of all Masters, Sayyiduna Muhammad, the Messenger of Allah, the Pride of Arabs and non-Arabs, the Hashimi, the Makki-Madani, Divine Blessings be upon him, with the reward that meets his most High Status. May Allah send great rewards to my early Masters of Ahlul-Bayt, who have been spiritually enlightening me and guiding me throughout my life, especially my great grandfathers Imam Husain and Imam Ali ibn Abi Talib and my great grandmother Lady (Sayyida) Fatima Az-zahraa, Divine Blessings be upon them all.

I am immensely grateful to my God-fearing Masters who have had immense favours upon me. I can only express my gratitude to them by praying to Allah Almighty to bless them and reward them abundantly with the reward that meets His Generosity and Greatness. I am particularly grateful to the great saintly scholars who have enlightened me with their profound knowledge, saintly wisdom and ever-flowing spiritual provision, especially to my Master Shaykh Muhammad In'amul-Hasan Kandahlawi, my Master Shaykh al-Hadith Muhammad Zakariya Kandahlawi, my Master Shaykh Mahmudul-Hasan Saharanpuri, my Master Shaykh Sa'eed Ahmad Khan Madani, my Master Shaykh Dr Owais ibn Abdullah Alhusaini, my Master and father Shaykh Abdussalam ibn Hashim Madani, my Master Shaykh Zubairul-Hasan Kandahlawi, my Master Shaykh Omar Phalampuri and my Master Shaykh Fazel Azeem Madani — may Allah be pleased with them all and grant them the highest of Heavenly Stations.

I would also like to thank my disciples who have contributed in any way to the production or distribution of my blessed books. May Allah reward them with Divine Love and high degrees. Amen.

CONTENTS

INTRODUCTION

Alhamdu-lillah - praise be to Allah Almighty, Lord of the worlds, who has blessed me with Divine openings for the development and enhancement of the seekers' spiritual wellbeing.

Blessings and Divine Prayers be upon our Master, Sayyiduna Muhammad, the Noble Arabian Makki-Madani, and upon his Noble Ahlul-Bayt (Household) - Sayyida Fatima, Sayyid Ali, Sayyid Al-Hasan and Sayyid Al-Husain, and upon their blessed descendants, including this poor slave, who have been Divinely chosen for the enlightenment and holy enrichment of the sincere servants of God.

My dear seeker! Know that the relationship of the seeker (murid) with his/her Lord is that of sincere and humble devotion to Allah Almighty and genuine dedication to His pure Path. In this blessed book, I have gathered for you prayers and supplications that help you acquire this devotion and attract the Help and Support of Allah to be on your side.

Whether you are my murid or a murid of any other true Master of any true Path, you can well benefit from this book to reach higher spiritual positions. Just remember me in your prayers. May Allah Almighty join us all together in His Divine Presence under the Flag of Light of Sayyiduna Muhammad, the last Messenger of Allah, and his blessed Ahlul-Bayt, Divine Blessings and Greetings be upon them all.

With my love and sincere prayers,

Sayyid Dr Al-Sharif Al-Husaini

THE BLESSED NAQSHABANDI SUPPLICATIONS
(NAQSHABANDI WIRD)

These Prayers are supplications that Imam Sayyid Muhammad Baha-uddin Naqshaband (Allah sanctified his soul) used to pray with on daily basis when calling upon Allah Almighty for all the spiritual and physical needs and gains that one can ask for. Allah Almighty inspired Imam Naqshaband to say these prayers due to his transparent and enlightened heart that was constantly devoted to the service of Allah. He was from the blessed descendants of the Holy Messenger (Bbuh). He was born on 14th of Muharram, 718 AH (18 March 1318 AD), in a village called Qasr Arifan near Bukhara, (now, in Uzbekistan).

As a seeker of Allah Almighty, you may read all these Naqshabandi Supplications together as one prayer at one time, which is best for you, or you could read them in four sessions over two days as I have arranged them for those who find difficulty in devoting enough time on one day.

FIRST MORNING:

In the Name of Allah, Most Gracious, Most Merciful. O Allah, You are The Divine King, The Ever-Living, The Self-Subsisting, The Truth, The Manifest. There is no God but You. You are my Lord. You Created me and I am Your slave; I will abide by Your Covenant and Command to the best of my capacity. I seek refuge in You from the evil I have committed. I acknowledge Your Favours upon me and I confess to You all my sins. I beg for Your Forgiveness, for certainly none can forgive sins but You.

Glory be to Allah. Praise be to Allah. There is no God but Allah. Allah is The Greatest. There is no power and no might except with Allah, The Most-High, The Great One. He is The First and He is The Last. He is The Apparent and The Hidden. He is All Knowing and All-Aware of all things. He is The Giver of life and death, and He is All-Competent at all things.

Praise be to You, Glorious One. Praise be to You, Most High. Praise be to You, Most Powerful. Praise be to You, Knower of all that is secret and all that is most concealed. Praise be to You, The One Who Resurrects beings on earth and in the heavens. Praise be to You, Controller of all creation. Praise be to You; You Have Predestined all wealth and earnings.

Praise be to You, Free from fault. Praise be to You, for You are Originator of time. You are Most Sublime. You are High above what they describe You to be. Praise be to You, for You grant freedom from Hell. Praise be to you, The Maker of all means and causes. Praise be to you, Ever-Living, Eternal. Praise be to You, my Lord and the Lord of all mankind. Our Lord! You created us with Your Power, and You Have Favoured us over many of Your creation. All Praise and Grace are due to You. All favours we have are due to You. You are Most Gracious, Most High. We seek Your Pardon and to You we repent.

You are The First, there was none before You. You are The Last, there is none after You. You are The Apparent, there is none like unto You. You are The Concealed, none can behold You. You are The One God; You have no need for partners. You are All-Powerful; You have no need for ministers. You are The Supreme Commander; You have no need for advisors. Say, O Allah! Lord of All Power and All Kingdom, You Empower whomever You Wish, and You Forbid power from whomever You Wish. You Honour whomever You Wish, and You Disgrace whomever You Wish: In Your Hands lie all good. Verily, You have all Power over all things.

You Make the night gain on the day, and You Make the day gain on the night; You Bring forth the living out of the dead, You Bring forth the dead out of the living; You give sustenance to whomever You Wish without count or measure.

O Most Compassionate in this life, Most Merciful in the hereafter! Glory be to You, The One, Veiled from the creation in this life. Glory be to You, The One, Distinguished with Grandeur and Pride.

Glory be to You, The Owner of all things. Glory be to You, The Honourable One with Power and Highness. O You, Knower of all that is in the heavens and in the earth! O You, Knower of all that which flutters in our hearts and of that within our chests! O You, Who Have Honoured the Two Holy Lands (Makkah and Madinah) over other towns and places! O You, Knower of all that is beneath the sand and the soil.

Glory be to You, Most High, You Are so Subtle that You Are not realised by our cognitive senses. Our Lord. You are Most

Blessed, Supreme; there is no Lord other than You, there is no Overpowering Deity except You. O Allah, You are The Kind Giver, The Source of Grace, The Grateful. I bear witness that You are God, Allah, there is no god but You. You are my Lord and the Lord of all things, the Creator of the heavens and the earth, Knower of the seen and the unseen, Most High, Most Glorious, The Supreme One.

Taa-seen-meem. Taa-seen. Allah has joined the two seas but with an invisible barrier in between, and they cannot transgress against one another.

"Allah. There is no god but He, The Living, The Self-Subsisting, The Eternal. No slumber nor sleep can seize Him. His are all things in the heavens and the earth. Who is there that can intercede in His Presence except with His Divine Permission! He Knows what is before them and what is behind them. Nor shall they compass aught of His knowledge except as He Wills. His Throne encompasses all the heavens and the earths. He never suffers any fatigue in guarding and preserving them, He is Most High, Supreme in Glory".

Haam-meem, Haam-meem, Haam-meem, Haam-meem, Haam-meem, Haam-meem, Haam-meem. "The matter has been fulfilled and victory has come - the enemies shall not be helped." "Haam-meem. The revelation of the Holy Book is from Allah, The Mighty, The All-Wise. He is The Forgiver of sins; He Accepts repentance, yet His Punishment is severe. He is The Kind Giver. There is no god but He: to Him is the final return." He is Able to do anything with His Own Power. He Governs as He Wills with His Might. No one can share His Power and He has no partner in His Kingdom.

Glory and Praise be to Allah. There is no Might except with Allah. Whatever Allah Wills, happens and that which He Does not Will cannot happen. I confirm that Allah Owns Power over all things and that Allah Has Full Knowledge of all things.

O Allah, do not kill us by Your Wrath, nor destroy us by leaving us engrossed in the passions of this world! Protect us so that Your punishment may never befall us! Glory be to You, The King, Most Holy. Glory be to You, Lord of Honour, Glory, Greatness, Power, Pride and Might! Glory be to The Majesty, The Truth, The Ever-Living, Who is never taken by sleep nor by death. The Pure One, The Holy One. You Are our Lord and The Lord of all angels and You are The Lord of the holy Spirit (Archangel Gabriel).

FIRST EVENING:

O Allah, grant us knowledge from Your Knowledge, make us have better understanding of what You Mean. Bless us with the Power of Your Help and Victory. O Allah, make me thank You, remember You, worship You, obey You and be totally devoted to You. Make me good-natured, soft hearted, supplicant to You and oft-repentant unto You.

O Allah, accept our repentance, wash away our wrongdoing and keep our tongues free from error. Take away all hatred that is within us and cleanse our hearts from all deceitfulness, corruption and cowardice.

O Allah, we seek refuge in You from sudden death, from moral corruption, from abandoning truth and from negligence. Protect us from amassing wealth, from all means of corruption and from all causes of our doom.

O Allah, grant us enough reverence for You that can save us from falling into error against You. Grant us enough obedience to You that allows us to enter Your Garden. Grant us enough certainty of Faith that reduces the misery of calamities in this world. O Allah, bless us to enjoy our hearing, our sight and our strength as long as we are destined to live, and make these blessings last for us to the end. O Allah, grant us power against those who oppress us, and support us against those who show enmity to us. O Allah, allow not calamity to come to our Faith, nor let this worldly life be our major concern, nor our share of knowledge. O Most Merciful One! Let us not be oppressed by those who show no mercy to us.

O Allah, we ask of Your Grace that by which You Guide our hearts, You Mend our torn pieces, You Unite our broken relations, You Cure our ill ones, You Purify our deeds and speech and You Inspire us with righteousness. O Allah, we ask You through Your Divine Power, through Your Oneness, through Your Dominant Glory and Your Extensive Mercy, to grant us light in our hearing, light in our eyesight, light in our eyes and light in our hearts. Grant us light in our senses, light in our souls and light in front of us.

O Allah, grant us more true knowledge, light and wisdom, and grant us plenty of the outer and inner bounties. Allah is

Sufficient for us for our Faith and for our worldly life. Allah is Sufficient for us for all of our worries and concerns.

Allah, Most Wise, Most Powerful, is Sufficient for us against those who wronged us. Allah, Most Merciful, is Sufficient for us at the time of death. Allah, Most Kind, is Sufficient for us when questioned in the grave.

"Allah is Sufficient for me: there is no God but He. On Him do I rely, Lord of The Throne". (Repeat 7 times)

O new morning and new day! (If in the evening: O new evening and new night!) Welcome, welcome to you. Welcome to the angel of witness: register what we say. In the name of Allah, Most Gracious, Most High, Most Loving, All Encompassing, Free to do with His creation as He Wills. He is closer to them than their jugular veins.

I know I have woken up this morning a believer in Allah: believing in my ultimate meeting with Him, confirming His rights over me, denying divinity to any other than Allah, and putting my complete trust in Allah alone.

We bear witness before Allah, and before His angels, His Prophets and Messengers, the Bearers of His Throne and before all of His creation, that there is no other god beside Allah and that our Master, Muhammad, is His Servant and Messenger. We bear witness that Heaven is true, the Fire is true, the Sacred Spring (HawD) is true, the Messenger's Intercession is true, questioning in the grave is true, the two Angels of the grave, Munkar and Nakeer, are true, that Your Promise is true, that the Last Hour is undoubtedly coming, and that Allah resurrects those in the graves. On this belief, we shall live and die, and with this belief, we shall be resurrected, and God willing, we shall not suffer any torture.

O Allah! We have wronged ourselves, forgive us all our sins, the major and the minor sins, for surely, none can forgive them except You. Guide us to the best of manners, for none can guide us to the best of manners except You. My Lord! Here I am forever Yours; all good is with You. From You do we ask for pardon and to You do we repent. We have believed in Your Messenger and in Your Holy Book.

O Allah, decorate our faces with modesty in Your Presence, and fill our hearts with happiness with You. O Allah, make me generous and noble, and do not make me stingy, a frequent sinner, a reporter gossip, arrogant or corruptive. O Allah, we seek refuge in You from excessive eating and excessive talking, from extreme worry and sadness, from pride, from living in hardship, from mistrust, from intoxicants, from greed, from laziness, from falsehood, from evil temptations and from living in misery.

O Allah, make the beginning of this day (or, "the beginning of this night") righteous, and the middle of it prosperous and the end of it success. O Allah, make the beginning of it full of mercy, the middle of it free from need of worldly things, and the end of it filled with honour. O Allah, make our life a blissful life, give us happiness in our time here, and give us plentiful provision that is beneficial for us.

O Allah, pardon us with Your Pardon, and be kind to us with Your Kindness. Glory and praise be to You. I am incapable of praising You the way You deserve to be praised. You are praiseworthy in the manner that You have Praised Yourself. Those are honoured who seek Your Protection. Your Tribute is most great. Your soldiers are never defeated. Your Promise is never broken; there is no god but You.

SECOND MORNING:

Glory be to You, The Worshiped One: we have not worshiped You as You deserve to be worshiped. Glory be to You, The Known One: we have not known You in the right manner You ought to be known. Glory be to You, Most Remembered One: we have not remembered You as You deserve to be remembered. Glory be to You, The Most Thanked One: we have not been thankful to You as You deserve to be thanked. O Allah! Grant us the proper manner to thank You for the favours that you have bestowed upon us.

You are God, Whose Powerful Attributes are High above human attributes. No partner has witnessed You when You created the creation, and there was no equal being to You who could prevent You from creating the souls You created.

O Allah! We seek refuge in You from tearless eyes, from hearts that do not tremble with Your reverence, from knowledge that is not beneficial to us, from egos that are never satisfied, from unanswered prayers and from dire poverty.

O Allah! Allow us to realise and understand Your Concealed Knowledge. Clothe us with the garments of Your Light. Submerse us in the ocean of spiritual subtleties, and shower us with the blessings of knowing You. O Light of Lights! O Most Kind, Concealer of sins! We ask You to send Your Blessings upon our Master, Sayyiduna Muhammad, the guiding light of all prophets and friends of Allah, the bright full moon to all the pure ones, the shining sun to both mankind and spirits, the radiance for both the East and the West. We beg You to raise our existence to be in the sphere of Divine Knowledge, and to secure our presence in the Station of Perfection.

O Allah, O Light! O You through Whose Command the sky was built, through Whose Power the earth was laid down, through Whose Wisdom the mountains were fixed firm, and through Whose Favour the sun and the moon were granted light.

We ask You by Your Name through Which the sun and the bright planets have been illuminated, and the heavens have been brightened, to give us a protective shield against all harm, and an overwhelmingly brilliant light that blind the eyes. Allah alternates the Night and the Day: verily in this reality is a great sign for those who have true insight.

Ta-Seen, Ta-Seen-Meem. We seek refuge in Allah The Magnificent from time-wasting instruments, from lying and slandering, from the prohibited things, from deceit, from the oppression of people, from the evil plots of the corrupt people, from the tribulations that emerge during the day or during the night, and from the horrors of torture in both this world and the hereafter.

O Guardian, guard us from all harm. O Protector, Most High, Most Eminent, The One beside Whom there is no other god. No one except You knows how You truly are. O Allah, Ever-Living, Self-Existing, The Truth, Sufficient Protector, The One, Indivisible One, The Distinguished, Self-Subsisting, Giver, Opener and Source of life and death.

Peaceful salutation is a Word from The Lord, Most Merciful. Allah will Suffice you as against others, for He is All-Hearing, All-Knowing.

He is God, Allah, there is no god but He: The Compassionate, The Merciful, The Sovereign, The Holy, The All-Peace, The

Source of Security, The Perfect Guardian, The Almighty, The Compeller, The Supreme, The Creator, The Originator, The Designer of forms, The Oft-Forgiving, The Dominant, The All-Giving, The All-Provider, The Opener, The All-Knowing, The Causer of compression, The Causer of expansion, The Abaser, The Exalter, The Giver of honour, The Giver of disgrace, The All-Hearing, The All-Seeing, The Judge, The Just, The Subtle, The All-Aware, The All-Clement, The All-Glorious, The Forgiver, The Thankful, The Sublime, The Great, The Protector, The Sustainer, The Reckoner, The Omnipotent,

The All-Generous, The Watchful, The One Who Answers prayers, The All-Comprehending, The All-Wise, The All-Loving, The Majestic, The Resurrector, The All-Witness, The Truth, The Universal Trustee, The All-Strong, Unyielding in Power, The True Friend, The Praiseworthy, The Reckoner, The Originator, The Restorer, The Giver of Life, The Life-Taker, The Ever-Living, The Eternal, The Wealthy, The Most Noble, The One, The Everlasting Refuge, The Powerful, The Prevailing, The Promoter, The Detainer, The First, The Last, The Manifest, The Hidden, The Protector.

He is The All-Exalted, The Beneficent, The Acceptor of Repentance, The Avenger, The Forgiving, The Gentle, The Lord of the Kingdom, The Lord of Majesty and Generosity, The Lord of Justice, The Gatherer, The Self-Sufficient, The Enricher, The Withholder, The Afflicter, The Beneficent, The Light, The Guide, The Innovator, The Everlasting, The Inheritor, The Righteous, The Forbearing. Nothing is like unto Him, He is The All-Hearing, The All-Seeing. Allah is sufficient for us.

He is The Best Trustee, The Best Disposer of affairs, The Best Protective Friend and the Best Supporter. Our Lord, Your forgiveness do we seek, and to You we shall return.

O my Lord, Ever Living without demise, Most Persistent without decay, The Divine Director without assistants, turn all difficulties into ease for us and for our parents. O Allah, nothing can deprive us of what You Have Given us and nothing can give us what You Have Denied us. Nothing can reject what You have Willed, and nothing can change what You Have Decreed. No one can guide the one You Have Mislead, and no one can mislead the one You Have Guided. No one can make easy what You Have Made difficult, and no one can make difficult what You Have made Easy. No one can benefit from their good deeds except if they are accepted by You.

Glory be to my Great High Lord, The Reckoner, The All-Ruler, The All Just, The All-Watchful, The All-Great, The Sublime, The One Who Answers prayers, The Wealthy, The Righteous, The Most Patient, The Almighty, The Equitable, The Giver, The Withholder.

There is no god but Allah, The Divine Trustee, The All-Witness. There is no god but Allah, The Unyielding in Power, The Majestic. There is no god but Allah, The Absolute in Wealth, The True Friend. There is no god but Allah, The Most Noble, The Exalted.

We have prepared for every horror: la ilaha illallah "There is no God but Allah", and for every favour: alhamdu-lillah "Praise be to Allah", and for every evil eye: subhan-allah "Glory be to Allah", and for every difficulty hasbiy-allah "Allah is Sufficient Power for me", and for every misery: masha-allah "Everything is the Will of Allah", and for every fate and destiny: tawakkaltu 'alallah "I rely only on Allah", and for every calamity: innaa-lillah "we belong to Allah", and for every act of obedience and disobedience: la Hawla walaa quwwata illa-billah "There is no power nor means of help except by Allah", and for every need: ista'antu billah "I seek the Support of Allah".

"O Allah, this morning (or "evening"), we bear witness before You and before Your angels, Your Prophets, Your Messengers, and before all of Your creation, that You are The True God Alone, without any partners, and that our Master, Muhammad, is Your servant and messenger". (Repeat 4 times).

In The Name of Allah, The Curer, He is Allah. In The Name of Allah, The All-Sufficient, He is Allah. In The Name of Allah, The Healer, He is Allah.

"In the name of Allah, with Whose Name nothing in the heavens or in the earth can harm us, He is All-Seeing, All-Knowing." (Repeat 3 times). Surely, Allah is The Best Protector, Most Merciful.

SECOND EVENING:

O Giver of Life, grant us a virtuous life: in health and in safety, both in this life and in the next; You are certainly Able to do anything.

"The Power of Allah encompasses them from all directions. Surely, this is the Glorious Quran, in the Heavenly Tablet Preserved! Guard strictly your prayers, and take extra care of the Middle Prayer; and stand before Allah in a devout condition. There is no soul but has a protector over it, and Allah is the Best of Protectors."

"O Divine Protector, Protect us." (Repeat 3 times)

Then, after the distress that befell you, He Sent down calm on a band of you overcome with slumber, while another band was stirred to anxiety by their own feelings, moved by wrong suspicions of Allah: suspicions due to ignorance.

They said, "What affair is this of ours?" Say, "Indeed, this affair is wholly of Allah." They hide in their hearts what they dare not reveal to you. They say, 'If we had the power to do anything with this affair, we would not have been in the slaughter here.' Say, 'Even if you had remained in your own homes, those for whom death was decreed would certainly have come forth to the places of their death;' but that Allah may test what is in your chests and purge what is in your hearts. For Allah knows well the deepest secrets in your hearts. Those who say, "Our Lord! We have indeed believed: forgive us, then, our sins, and save us from the agony of the Fire of Hell.

Those who show patience, firmness and self-control; who are true in word and in deed; who worship devoutly; who spend in the Way of Allah; and who spend the night praying for forgiveness. There is no god but He: That is the witness of Allah, His angels, and of those endued with knowledge, standing firm on justice. Surely, there is no god but He, The Exalted in Power, The Wise. With Allah, the true Religion is Islam. Thus, glorify Allah, when you reach eventide and when you rise in the morning; to Him be praise, in the heavens and on earth; and in the evening and when the day begins to decline.

It is He Who brings out the living from the dead, and brings out the dead from the living, and Who gives life to the land after it is dead: and thus will you too be brought out from the dead.

I put my trust in Allah, my Lord and your Lord! There is not a moving creature, but He has full grasp of its forelock. Verily, it is my Lord Who is on the Straight Path. No reason have we why we should not put our trust in Allah. Indeed, He Has guided us to our good ways. We shall certainly bear with patience all the hurt that you may cause us. For those who put their trust should put their trust in Allah. Say, "Nothing will happen to us except what Allah has decreed for us: He is our Protector", and on Allah, the Believers should put their trust. There is no living creature on earth but its sustenance depends on Allah. He knows the time and place of its definite abode and its temporary deposit: All is recorded in a clear Register. How many a creature that does not carry its own sustenance but Allah provides it its sustenance and the same for you, for He is The All-Hearing, All Knowing.

What Allah, out of His Mercy, Does Bestow upon mankind, none can withhold: what He Does Withhold, none can grant, apart from Him; He is The Exalted in Power, All-Wise. If indeed you ask them who it is that created the heavens and the earth, they would surely say, "Allah".

Say, "Can you not see then? The things that you invoke besides Allah, can they, if Allah wills some Penalty on me, remove His Penalty? Or if He Wills some grace for me, can they prevent His Grace?" Say, "Sufficient is Allah for me! In Him trust those who put their trust." Allah Has Sent it but a message of hope for you, and an assurance to your hearts - there is no true help except from Allah. The Exalted, the Wise.

Kaaf-ha-yaa-'ayn-SaaD. Haa-meem. 'ayn-seen-qaaf: Suffice us with Your Power and have mercy upon us. He is Allah, The Able, The Dominant, The Manifest, The Concealed, The Originator, The Most Kind, The All-Aware. His Word is the Truth, and His will be the Dominion on the Day when the Trumpet will be blown. He is All-Knowing of hidden and the seen; He is All Wise, Well Acquainted with all things.

I am in the Protection of Allah, The All-Strong, The Firm One, The Most Kind, The Subsisting, The Protector, The Ever Living. The One Who neither fatigue nor sleep can overtake Him. The Most Compassionate, The Most Kind. O Most Magnificent, Originator of the heavens and the earth, Ever Living, Eternal. O Possessor of Majesty and Honour, we ask You by Your Great Lordship to change our inner selves from that of the human nature and to raise our souls to be with Your high Angels.

"O Transformer of states and conditions, turn our condition into the best of conditions". (Repeat 3 times)

Glory and Praise be to You. I bear witness that there is no god but You. I beg for Your forgiveness and to You I do repent.

O Allah, send Your Blessings upon our Master, Muhammad; blessings that will be the means of our salvation from all the horrors and trauma of the Day of Judgment. Send upon him Blessings that will fulfill all of our needs and that which will purify us from all of our sins. Send upon him Blessings that will raise our stations to the highest of all stations. Send upon him Blessings that will raise us to the highest of virtuous destinations in this world and after death. Send abundant Blessings and Greetings upon him and upon his Family and Companions.

O Allah, send Your Blessings upon our Master, Muhammad, whose light preceded the existence of mankind, and whose coming to earth is mercy for all mankind. Allah, send upon him as many Blessings as the number of mankind who have passed away and the number of those who remain to come, and as many as those who are fortunate and as many as those who are wretched. O Allah, send upon Sayyiduna Muhammad continuous Blessings that encompass all the creation, Blessings that have no limit and that never stop and never end, the Blessings that You have already been sending upon him from time immemorial. Allah, send similar Blessings upon his Family, Ahlul-Bayt, and upon all of his Supporters. All praise be to Allah, Lord of the worlds.

PRAYER OF THE NAQSHABANDI CHAIN OF SAINTS

This is a special prayer for gaining heavenly openings and higher stations for the devoted seeker. In Arabic, it is called dua as-silsilah ash-sharifah, 'Prayer of the Blessed Chain'. It is recommended be recited in specific occasions: at the time of Naqshabandi initiation (bay'a or talqeen) when you are accepted by your Shaykh in the Naqshabandi Path (Tariqa), at the beginning of your daily heart zikr session, after completing the Naqshabandi Supplications (Wird), after the Khatm Khawagakan prayers, and at the time of dire need when you want relief from difficulties or cure from illnesses. This Blessed Prayer includes the names of all the Saints who inspired and taught millions of seekers throughout history on the Naqshabandi Path headed by the Master of all Masters, Sayyiduna Muhammad (Bbuh). Therefore, when a Naqshabandi murid prays to Allah Almighty with this prayer, the spiritual energy of all these Saints, including the Messenger of Allah (Bbuh) becomes directed to the reciter and thus transfer Divine Light and Faith to the seeker's heart and mind.

O Allah! I beg of You, I repent to You, I seek firmness, I seek mediation, I devote my direction, I beseech, I seek protection, I fortify myself, I seek healing, I seek learning, I seek understanding, I seek remembrance, I seek awareness, I seek spiritual training, I seek elevation, I seek heights, I seek arrival, and I seek nearness through Your Divine Secrets and through the Lights of Your Divine Manifestations that You have placed in these sublime Paths of our Masters and through the blessings of these Muslim saints (in the Siddiqiya Chain): Master Sayyid Al-Sharif Al-Husaini, Master Sayyid Owais Alhusaini, Master Sayyid Manzour Husain Sindi, Master Muhammad Mujtaba Khan, Master Hafez Waliyunnabi, Master Ahmad ibn Saeed, Master Abu Saeed progeny of Imam Rabbani, Master Abdullah Shah Ghulam, Master Habibullah Jani-Janan, Master Sayyid Noor Muhammad, Master Muhammad Saifuddin, Master Muhammad Ma'sum, Master Ahmad Farouqi, Master Muhammad Baqi-Billah, Master Muhammad Khawajah Amkanki, Master Muhammad Darwish, Master Muhammad Zahid, Master Ubeidullah Ahrar, Master Ya'qub Al-jarkhi, Master 'Ala-uddin 'Attaar, Master Sayyid Baha-uddin Naqshaband, Master Sayyid Ameer Kulal, Master Muhammad Baba Samasi, Master Azizan Nassaj Ramitni,

Master Mahmud Injir Faghnawi, Master Muhammad Arif Rayukari, Master Abdul-khaliq Ghajdawani, Master Yusuf Hamadani, Master Abu-Ali Al-fadhl Faramdi, Master Abul-Hasan Kharqani, Master Abu-Yazid Bistami, Master Ja'far AS-Sadiq, Master Al-qasim ibn Muhammad ibn Abu-Bakr, Master Salman Al-farisi, Master Abu-Bakr AS-Siddiq, and Master of all Masters, the Fountain of all goodness, Sayyiduna Muhammad, the last Messenger of Allah (Blessings be upon him); and through our Masters (in the Golden Chain): Master Sayyid Al-Sharif Al-Husaini, Master Sayyid Owais Alhusaini, Master Sayyid Manzour Husain Sindi, Master Muhammad Mujtaba Khan, Master Hafez Waliyunnabi, Master Ahmad ibn Saeed, Master Abu Saeed progeny of Imam Rabbani, Master Abdullah Shah Ghulam, Master Habibullah Jani-Janan, Master Sayyid Noor Muhammad, Master Muhammad Saifuddin, Master Muhammad Ma'sum, Master Ahmad Farouqi, Master Muhammad Baqi Billah, Master Muhammad Khawajah Amkanki, Master Muhammad Darwish, Master Muhammad Zahid, Master Ubeidullah Ahrar, Master Ya'qub Al-jarkhi, Master 'Ala-uddin 'Attaar, Master Sayyid Baha-uddin Naqshaband, Master Sayyid Ameer Kulal, Master Muhammad Baba Samasi, Master Azizan Nassaj Ramitni,

Master Mahmud Injir Faghnawi, Master Muhammad Arif Rayukari, Master Abdul-khaliq Ghajdawani, Master Yusuf Hamadani, Master Abu-Ali Al-fadhl Faramdi, Master Abul-qasim Al-jurjani, Master Abu-Uthman Maghribi, Master Abu-Ali Ruzhabari, Master Junaid Baghdadi, Master As-sariy As-saqati, Master Ma'ruf Al-karkhi, Master Sayyid Ali Ar-rida, Master Sayyid Musa Al-kazim, Master Sayyid Ja'far AS-Sadiq, Master Sayyid Muhammad Al-baqir, Master Sayyid Ali Zainul-'abideen, Master Sayyid Al-Husain ibn Ali, Master Sayyid Ali ibn Abi-Talib, Master of all Masters, the Fountain of all goodness, Sayyiduna Muhammad, the last Messenger of Allah (Blessings be upon him), and through our Master angels, Jibreel, Mikaeel and Israfeel, peace be upon them.

My Divine God, You are my Destination, and Your Pleasure is my purpose of life. Bless me with the gift of Loving You and knowing You. O Allah! I ask You through Your Honour, Glory, Beauty, Power, Sublimity and Greatness, and through the most inner secret of the secrets of Your Glorious Names, Your Noble Prophets, Your great Friends and Your nearest angels, and through the Truth of "la ilaha illallah – mohammadon rasoolollah", and with the Truth of this Holy Name, الله ALLAH, ALLAH, ALLAH, with the reality of the alif

(A), that is completely independent of the other letters, and with the reality of the two laam (LL) within which You have kept Your secrets, and with the reality of the ha (H) that encompasses and moves the stationary, the animate and the inanimate objects - that You bless me with beholding Your Glorious Face, that You fulfil my needs, that You open for me the doors of knowledge and secrets, that You overwhelm me with the blessings of the Glorious Throne, the Divine Seat and the Preserved Tablet, and that You manifest Yourself and Your Lights in my heart with all the levels of manifestation that You have bestowed upon Your Prophets and Your chosen friends, from Your Kindness and Generosity, O Most Gracious One. "There is no God but You, Glory be to You, I have been of the wrongdoers. Thus, We answered him and saved him from distress; such is what We do for the believers."

O Allah, I have thus submitted myself under the Muhammadan Spout, in my condition as worthless, lowly, sinner and seeking his intercession – make possible for me Your Divine Manifestations, Your angels' holy secrets, Your friends' sublime determinations, and Your beloved's Muhammadan spiritual flow.

"Had they come to You whenever they wronged themselves, and sought forgiveness of Allah and sought your request for forgiveness on their behalf, they would have found Allah Most Forgiving, Most Merciful". "Our Lord! Grant us the merit of this world and the merit of the hereafter, and save us from torture of the Fire". "Our Lord! Save our hearts from deviation now that You have guided us; grant us a Blessing from You, for You are the Absolute Donor". "Our Lord! Forgive me, my parents and all the believers on the Day of Judgement". "Our Lord! Forgive us and forgive our brethren who had died as believers and do not let our hearts have grudges against the believers – our Lord, You are Most Clement, Gracious". "Glory be to Your Lord, the Lord of Honour, He is far above what they claim; Greetings be upon the Messengers; and Praise is for Allah, the Lord of the worlds".

THE NIGHT SUPPLICATIONS (THE NIGHT WIRD) OF SAYYID AL-SHARIF AL-HUSAINI

This blessed prayer is a Divine opening to me. I pray it in my supplications to the Almighty during my night worship. I would recommend it for every seeker and every Muslim to communicate with Allah Almighty through this prayer during their night worship. Night worship begins from after Isha Prayer and ends at the beginning time of Fajr Prayer. The best part of the night to witness Divine Manifestation is the last third of the night.

I seek refuge in Allah from the cursed devil. In the Name of Allah, All-Gracious, All-Merciful. "He called from under layers of darkness, 'there is no God but You, Glory be to You, I am certainly one of the wrongdoers'."

In the Name of Allah. Glory be to Allah. Praise be to Allah. There is no God but Allah. Allah is Greatest. There is no ability nor power save from the Power of Allah. I seek forgiveness of Allah, Most Forgiving. I seek concealment of my faults by the Concealer, during the darkness of the night and during daylight. I am hopeful in the kindness of the Most Kind, All-Knowing, and in the protection of the Capable Protector. "There is no God but You, Glory be to You, I am certainly one of the wrongdoers". "There is no God but You, Glory be to You, I am certainly one of the wrongdoers". "There is no God but You, Glory be to You, I am certainly one of the wrongdoers", but You are All Merciful.

My Lord! Send Your Blessings upon the Seal of all Your prophets, who is the best of those who stand and prostrate to You, who is the holder of continuous light and flowing grace, the one of paramount beauty and supreme generosity; the Divinely gifted mercy, my Master Muhammad son of Abdullah; the Crown over my head, Messenger of Allah; the healer of my heart, Prophet of Allah; the light of my eyes, the beloved of Allah. My Lord, send further Blessings and greetings upon his noble family members, Ahlul-Bayt, who are the shining suns from the beginning of time to the end of time, and upon his companions, the guiding stars. O Allah, the Ever-Living, send

Your endless salutations upon them all, and bless them abundantly and endlessly.

"There is no God but You, Glory be to You, I am certainly one of the wrongdoers". My Lord! Truly, truly, and it is perfectly real that there is no God but You, Free from all defects.

How Glorious You are! How magnificent Your Governing Power is! I have wronged myself, and if You do not forgive me and show mercy to me, I will surely be a loser.

My Lord! I call upon You from under layers of darkness, when no one hears me but You! "There is no God but You, Glory be to You, I am certainly one of the wrongdoers". Glory be to You, the One, the Indivisible One, Self-Subsisting, Distinguished in greatness of Glory and in perfection of Beauty. Glory be to You, who was always there when there was none; and You will always be there when there will be none but You! You are surely needless of the creation. You are perfect in Truth. You are the true Destination even when there is not anyone to seek You. You are the Worshipped One even when there are no worshippers. You are the Creator even when there is no creation. There is none like unto You, nor opposite to You, nor anything similar to You. You are truly the Lord of the worlds.

My Lord! I call upon You from under layers of darkness, where no one sees me but You! "There is no God but You, Glory be to You, I am certainly one of the wrongdoers". O Amender of the broken ones! Amend what is broken in me. O Strong One! Have mercy upon my weakness. O Honourable One! Be gentle with my meekness. O Kind One! Be kind to my servitude to You. "There is no God but You, Glory be to You, I am certainly one of the wrongdoers". I have wronged myself, but You are All Merciful.

My Lord! I call upon You from under layers of darkness, when I have no other Lord but You. I beg You through Your Love for Your beloved, Ahmad, my Master Muhammad, the honoured one, and through Your Love for his household and his righteous supporters, to accept my repentance in such a manner that I may never disobey You again. I beg You to wipe out from my record of deeds, from my heart, from my memory, and from all existence, every sin I have ever committed, every mistake I have ever made and every evil I have ever done, for You are All Generous, All Kind, so that I may not remember anything but Your Favours upon me and

Your Compassion for me. "There is no God but You, Glory be to You, I am certainly one of the wrongdoers", but You are All Merciful.

My Lord, I call upon You from under layers of darkness, and I am the poor one indeed! "There is no God but You, Glory be to You, I am certainly one of the wrongdoers". Allahu, Allahu, Allah, Allah is my Lord – He is my Supporter, He is Sufficient for me, He is my Saviour, He is my Ally, He is with me and He is full of mercy for me. Allahu, Allahu, Allah. O Allah, You are the Most Compassionate, of Eternal Existence. You have created me in weakness, and made me live in weakness. I confess to You my overwhelming shortcomings. I apologise to You from my scarce presence. I complain to You from my fear of my doom.

"He called from under layers of darkness, 'there is no God but You, Glory be to You, I am certainly one of the wrongdoers'." My Lord! I am hopeful in Your Vast Mercy. Please accept my regret, for, due to my poverty, I am full of hope in Your Compassion. Grant me with the virtue of Your Grants which You give freely without count. My sins do not cause any loss to You and my acts of worship do not cause You any gain. My faults do not harm You, and my virtues do not benefit You in the least, You are the Hope of Your loyal slaves. "There is no God but You, Glory be to You, I am certainly one of the wrongdoers", but You are Most Merciful.

"He called from under layers of darkness, 'there is no God but You, Glory be to You, I am certainly one of the wrongdoers'." My Lord! With Your vast Mercy You forgive every fall and with Your encompassing Virtue You fulfil the needs and prevent calamities, and with Your great Favour You raise Your servants to high stations. O Allah! I am the poor and needy one indeed, the humbled one in Your presence. Please shower me with Your Mercy, grant me Your Virtue and Favour as befits Your Grandeur, O One with Perfect Attributes.

O Allah! You are All-Forgiving All-Kind, You love to pardon so pardon me, my parents and my teachers, O Most Kind, Most Compassionate. "There is no God but You, Glory be to You, I am certainly one of the wrongdoers", but You are Most Merciful.

O Allah, sanctify and bless my Master Muhammad, the trustworthy one, who is most compassionate and merciful with the believers, in such a manner that You grant me through this Prayer perfect firmness on true faith, save me through it from all harms, raise me through it to the highest of Divine stations, and enable me through it to achieve the best of all good things. O Allah, also sanctify and bless his family, Ahlul-Bayt, the holders of all virtues, for You are the One who answers prayers.

"There is no God but You, Glory be to You, I am certainly one of the wrongdoers", "There is no God but You, Glory be to You, I am certainly one of the wrongdoers", "There is no God but You, Glory be to You, I am certainly one of the wrongdoers". Have mercy upon me, for You are the Most Merciful.

NAQSHABANDI DEVOTIONS (AKHTAM) FOR FULFILLING ONE'S NEEDS

These are various akhtam (devotions) to be used for seeking the Help of Allah in removing serious difficulties and calamities and for fulfilling one's needs. Each khatm (Devotion) consists of a series of deeds, including the main Khatm phrase which should be repeated 500 time at one time. It should then be followed by further series of deeds to complete the Devotion. The following steps, from 1 to 6, are common steps in all the Devotions prior to the Khatm phrase:

1. Pray two rakaat, reading Surat Fatiha once and ayat Alkursi 7 times in each rakaa

2. Do istighfar (seek forgiveness) by repeating "Allah! Forgive me!" 25 times

3. Recite the following prayer with devotion:

"O Originator of all causes! O stirrer of hearts and eye sights! O Guide of the bewildered! O Saviour of those seeking help, save me! My Lord, I am relying on You, I have rested all my affairs on You, O Opener of good ways, O Giver, O Benefactor, O Expander. The Blessings of Allah be upon the best of His creation, Sayyiduna Muhammad, and upon his Household and his Companions."

يَا مُسَبِّبَ الْأَسْبَابِ. يَا مُقَلِّبَ الْقُلُوبِ وَالْأَبْصَارِ. يَا دَلِيلَ الْمُتَحَيِّرِينَ. يَا غِيَاثَ الْمُسْتَغِيثِينَ. أَغِثْنِي. تَوَكَّلْتُ عَلَيْكَ يَا رَبِّي. وَفَوَّضْتُ أَمْرِي إِلَيْكَ. يَا فَتَّاحُ. يَا وَهَّابُ. يَا بَاسِطُ. وَصَلَّى اللهُ عَلَى خَيْرِ خَلْقِهِ سَيِّدِنَا مُحَمَّدٍ وَعَلَى آلِهِ وَصَحْبِهِ أَجْمَعِينَ.

4. Engage into the blessed Connection of Shaykh (Rabitah Sharifa)

5. Read Surat Fatiha 7 times

6. Read these Salawat 100 times (either in English or Arabic):

"O Allah, send Your Blessings and Greetings upon our Master Muhammad and upon his Household"

Allahomma Salli wa-sallim 'ala sayyidina moHammad-in wa-aali sayyidina moHammad

Now, choose one of the six Seal Prayers (akhtam) below and repeat it in the given number of times, then follow the instructions to complete the khatm zikr:

I. KHATM OF MASTER MUHAMMAD BAHAUDDIN NAQSHABAND (RA):

"O Allah, who can change conditions, change our condition to the best of conditions" (500 times)

Allahomma ya mobaddilal-aHwaal, baddil Haalanaa ila aHsani Haal

(اللَّهُمَّ يَا مُبَدِّلَ الْأَحْوَالْ بَدِّلْ حَالَنَا إِلَى أَحْسَنِ حَالْ)

---

2. KHATM OF MASTER AHMAD FAROUQI (RA) AND MASTER MUHAMMAD MUJTABA KHAN (RA):

"There is no power save that empowered by Allah" (500 times), and every time you complete 100 times, say: "There is no power save that empowered by Allah, Most High, Most Glorious"

la Hawla wala-qowwata illa billah –

la Hawla wala-qowwata illa billahil 'aliyyil 'aZeem

(لَا حَوْلَ وَلَا قُوَّةَ إِلَّا بِاللهِ) (لَا حَوْلَ وَلَا قُوَّةَ إِلَّا بِاللهِ الْعَلِيِّ الْعَظِيْمِ)

3. KHATM OF MASTER MUHAMMAD MA'SUM (RA):

"O One with Most Hidden subtleties, help us with Your hidden subtlety!" (500 times)

Yaa khafiyyal-alTaaf adriknaa bi-luTfikal-khafi

(يَا خَفِيَّ الْأَلْطَافْ أَدْرِكْنَا بِلُطْفِكَ الْخَفِي)

---

4. KHATM OF MASTER ABDULLAH DAHLAWI (RA):

"O Most Compassionate, O Most Merciful, O More Merciful than all the merciful ones! Send Blessings upon Sayyiduna Muhammad" (500 times)

Ya raHmaano, ya raHeemo, ya arHamar-raaHimeen, Salli 'ala sayyidina muHammad

(يَا رَحْمَنُ يَا رَحِيْمُ، يَاأَرْحَمَ الرَّاحِمِيْن، صَلِّ عَلَى سَيِّدِنَا مُحَمَّد)

---

5. KHATM OF MASTER ABDUL-KHALIQ GHAJDAWANI (RA) - also known as the "Major Khatm", used in situations of major difficulties:

1. Read Surat Fatiha, together with bismillahir-raHmanir-raHeem, 7 times

2. Read Surat Inshirah 79 times

3. Read Surat Ikhlas 1001 times

6. KHATM OF MASTER ABDUL-QADIR JILANI (RA):

"Allah is Sufficient for us, He is the Best Trustee" (500 times)

Hasbonal-laaho wa-ni'mul-wakeel

(حَسْبُنَا اللّٰهُ وَنِعْمَ الْوَكِيْل)

Then follow these steps:

1. Read the following Salawat 100 times

"O Allah, send Your Blessings and Greetings upon our Master Muhammad and upon his Household"

Allahomma Salli wa-sallim 'ala sayyidina moHammad-in wa-aali sayyidina moHammad

2. Gift the rewards of all the above to the blessed souls of the saints in both Naqshabandi chains, reading their blessed names from your Shaykh upwards

3. Read the following prayer:

"O Allah make us from those related to them and dependent upon them. O Allah give us ability to that which You love and pleases You, O Most Merciful. Protect us from the evil self-thoughts and from the devilish desires. Purify us from human lowliness and Sanctify us with the sanctity of love and truthfulness. O Allah show us the Truth as truth and enable us to follow it. And show us falsehood as false and enable us to abstain from it, O Most Merciful One. O Allah, I beg You to revive our hearts, souls and bodies with the light of Knowing You, connecting to You, and with Your Divine Manifestations, always and forever O Allah.

اللّٰهُمَّ اجْعَلْنَا مِنَ المَحْسُوبِينَ عَلَيْهِمْ ۞ وَمِنَ الْمَنْسُوبِينَ إِلَيْهِمْ ۞ وَوَفِّقْنَا لِمَا تُحِبُّهُ وَتَرْضَاهُ ۞ يَا أَرْحَمَ الرَّاحِمِينَ ۞ أَجِرْنَا مِنَ الْخَوَاطِرِ النَّفْسَانِيَّةِ ۞ وَاحْفَظْنَا مِنَ الشَّهَوَاتِ الشَّيْطَانِيَّةِ ۞ وَطَهِّرْنَا مِنَ القَاذُورَاتِ الْبَشَرِيَّةِ ۞ وَصَفِّنَا بِصَفَاءِ الْمَحَبَّةِ الصِّدِّيقِيَّةِ ۞ اللّٰهُمَّ أَرِنَا الْحَقَّ حَقّاً

وَارْزُقْنَا اتِّبَاعَهُ ۞ وَأَرِنَا الْبَاطِلَ بَاطِلاً وَارْزُقْنَا اجْتِنَابَهُ ۞ يَا أَرْحَمَ الرَّاحِمِينَ ۞ اللَّهُمَّ إِنِّي أَسْأَلُكَ أَنْ تُحْيِيَ قُلُوبَنَا وَأَرْوَاحَنَا وَأَجْسَامَنَا بِنُورِ مَعْرِفَتِكَ ۞ وَوَصْلِكَ وَتَجَلِّيَاتِكَ ۞ دَائِماً بَاقِياً يَا اللهُ ۞

4. Pray for your need by repeating what you want from Allah Almighty 3 to 7 times

5. Read the following prayer (3-7 times):

"O Allah, the One who fulfils wishes, the One who suffices all needs, the Protector from calamities, the Healer of illnesses, the Raiser of heavenly stations and the One who answers prayers, O Most Merciful One."

اللَّهُمَّ يَا قَاضِيَ الْحَاجَاتِ، يَا كَافِيَ الْمُهِمَّاتِ، يَا دَافِعَ الْبَلِيَّاتِ، يَا شَافِيَ الْأَمْرَاضِ، يَا رَافِعَ الدَّرَجَاتِ، يَا مُجِيبَ الدَّعَوَاتِ، يَاأَرْحَمَ الرَّاحِمِينَ ۞

6. Read these concluding Salawat:

"O Allah! Send abundant Blessings and Greetings upon our Master Muhammad and upon his Household and Companions by which You deliver us from every fear and calamity, fulfil our every need, purify us from every sin and error, raise us to the highest of stations, and make us attain the highest degrees of goodness in this life and in the life after death."

اَللّٰهُمَّ صَلِّ عَلَى سَيِّدِنَا مُحَمَّدٍ صَلَاةً تُنْجِينَا بِهَا مِنْ جَمِيعِ الْأَهْوَالِ وَالْآفَاتِ ۞ وَتَقْضِي لَنَا بِهَا جَمِيعَ الْحَاجَاتِ ۞ وَتُطَهِّرُنَا بِهَا مِنْ جَمِيعِ السَّيِّئَاتِ ۞ وَتَرْفَعُنَا بِهَا عِنْدَكَ أَعْلَى الدَّرَجَاتِ وَتُبَلِّغُنَا بِهَا أَقْصَى الْغَايَاتِ ۞ مِنْ جَمِيعِ الْخَيْرَاتِ فِي الْحَيَاةِ وَبَعْدَ الْمَمَاتِ ۞ وَعَلَى آلِهِ وَصَحْبِهِ وَسَلِّمْ تَسْلِيمًا كَثِيرًا ۞

Finally, remember to pray for the author of this book, Sayyid Al-Sharif Al-Husaini, in gratitude for the favour of Allah over you through the author's guidance.

HOLY VERSES OF THE SECRET OF QAF

These are five holy ayat (verses) containing the power of the Arabic letter ق "Qaf" in Holy Quran, which is repeated ten times in each of these verses. In addition to great heavenly reward for reciting it, this blessed zikr is beneficial for protection from all harms and enemies as well as for elevation in spiritual status. Recite each holy verse once and read the attached zikr 3 times. After you recite all the five holy verses and their attached zikr, read the related Prayer once at the end. It is best that you recite the verses in their original Arabic pronunciation. But, if you find it very difficult, read the translation until you have learnt their Arabic recitation.

VERSE I

"Look at that community from the Progeny of Israel, after Moses, when they said unto one of their prophets: Raise up for us a king so that we can fight in the cause of Allah, and he replied: Would you then turn away from fighting if fighting were to be prescribed upon you? They said: and why should we not fight in the cause of Allah when we have been cast out from our homes and our children (families)? Yet, when fighting was prescribed upon them, they all turned away, save a very few of them. Allah is fully Aware of the wrongdoers". (Sura Al-baqara: 246)

(Allah is fully Aware and Capable of whatever He Wills)
(repeat 3 times)

Transliteration:

alum tara ilal-mala-i min banee israeela, min ba'di moosa, izh qaloo linabiyyin lahumu-b'ath lana malikan, nuqaatil fee sabeelil-lahi, qaala hal 'asaytom in kutiba 'alaykumul-qitaalu allaa tuqatiloo? qaaloo wama-lana allaa nuqatila fee sabeelil-lahi waqad okhrijna min diyarina wa-abnaa-ina! falammaa kotiba 'alayhimol-qitaalo tawalluw illaa qaleelam minhom, wul-laaho 'aleemom bizhaalimeen.

'aleemon qadeeron 'alaa maa yoreed (repeat 3 times)

VERSE 2

"Verily, Allah heard the speech of those who said, "Allah is poor and we are rich!" We shall keep their saying in register along with their wrongful slaying of the Prophets and We shall command: Taste the torture of burning (in Hell)". (Sura Aal Imran:181)

(Allah is All-Powerful! He does not need a helper)
(repeat 3 times)

Transliteration:

laqad sami'al-laaho qawlul-lazheena qaaloo innal-laaha faqeeron wanuHno aghniyaa, sanuktobo maa qaaloo, waqutlahomol-ambiya-a bighayri haqqin, wanaqoolo zooqoo 'azhabul-Hareeq.

Qawiyyon laa yaHtaajo ilaa mo'een (repeat 3 times)

VERSE 3

"Look at those who were told to hold back their hands (from fight), to establish prayers and spend in charity, but when the command of fighting was issued to them, a group of them feared men as they feared Allah, or even more than they feared Allah, and they said: "Our Lord! Why have You commanded us to fight?! Can You not grant us respite to another time near?" Say: "Short is the enjoyment of this world; the Hereafter is best for those who do right: never will you be dealt with unjustly in the very least!

(He is Overpowering over every transgressor and sinner)
(repeat 3 times)

Transliteration:

alam tara ilal-lazheena qeela lahom koffoo aydiyakom wa-aqeemos-salaata wa-aatoz-zakaata, falummaa kotiba 'alayhimol-qitaalo izha fareeqom-minhom yukhshuwnan-naasa ka-khashyatil-laahi aw ashadda khushyatun, waqaaloo rabbanaa lima katubta 'alaynul-qitaala, lawlaa akh-khurtanaa ilaa ajalin qareeb, qol mata'od-donyaa qaleelon wul-aakhirato khayron li-manit-taqaa, walaa toZlamoona fateelaa.

Qahhaaron limun Taghaa wa-'aSaa (repeat 3 times)

VERSE 4

"And relate to them the true story of the two sons of Adam, when each of them presented a sacrifice (to Allah), and it was accepted from one but not from the other. Said the latter: "I will surely kill you." "Surely", said the other, "Allah accepts only from the righteous". (Sura Al-maida: 27)

(You are Divine, You guide whoever You will)

(repeat 3 times)

Transliteration:

Wutlo 'alayhim nababnai aadama bilHaqqi izh qarrabaa qorbanan, fatoqobbila min aHadihimaa walum yotaqabbal minal-aakhari, qaala la-aqtolannaka, qaala innamaa yataqubbalol-laaho minal-mottaqeen.

Qoddooson yahdee mun yashaa (repeat 3 times)

VERSE 5

Say, who is the Lord of the heavens and the earth? Say, He is God (Allah); then say, "Have you then taken (for worship) allies other than Him, who cannot cause themselves benefit nor harm?!" Ask them, "Are the blind equal with those who see?! Or are the depths of darkness equal with Light?" Have they assigned to Allah partners who have created as He has created so that they got confused between His creation and their creation?! Say: "Allah is the Creator of all things: He is the One God, the Supreme."

(You are Self-Subsisting! You grant power and wealth to whomever You wish) (repeat 3 times)

Transliteration:

qol mur-rubbos-samaawati wularDi, qolil-laah, qol afuttakhazhtom min doonihi awliya-a laa yumlikoona lianfosihim naf'aw-walaa Durrun, qol hul yustawil-a'maa wulbaSeero, um hul tastawiZ-Zolomaato wunnooro, um ja'aloo lillaahi shoraka-a khalaqoo ka-khulqihi fatashaabahulkhulqo 'alayhim, qolil-laaho khaaliqo kolli shuy'in, wahowulwaaHidol-qahhaar.

Quyyoomon yurzoqo mun yashaa-ul-qowwata wul-ghinaa

(repeat 3 times)

PRAYER OF THE VERSES OF THE SECRET OF QAF:

(You can pray this Prayer in English or in Arabic)

"Our God, Whose favours cannot be counted, Whose commands cannot be disobeyed, Who broke the sea asunder for Moses with the means of a staff, we ask You by the one in whose hand the pebbles recited Divine Praises (Prophet Muhammad) and by each letter of the Holy Quran, that You make these holy verses a chaining prison and an obliterative sea, and grant us guards of seventy-thousand angels. O Allah! Whoever wants to harm me with any evil or with any sneaky plot or betrayal, burn his chest, destroy his plots and turn his tricks to be against himself, for You are Supreme over everything. O Allah, send Your Blessings upon Your Messenger, Muhammad, and upon his family and companions."

اللّهُمَّ يَا مَنْ نِعَمُهُ لا تُحْصَى، وَيَا مَنْ أَمْرُهُ لا يُعْصَى، يَا مَنْ فَلَقَ الْبَحْرَ لِمُوسَى بِالْعَصَا. نَسْأَلُكَ بِمَنْ سَبَّحَ فِي كَفِّهِ الْحَصَى، وَبِالْقُرْآنِ الْعَظِيمِ حَرْفاً حَرْفاً. أَنْ تَجْعَلَ هَذِهِ الآيَاتِ حَبْساً حَابِساً، وَبَحْراً طَامِساً، وَبِسَبْعِينَ أَلْفٍ مِنَ الْمَلائِكَةِ حَارِساً. اللّهُمَّ مَنْ أرَادَنِي بِسُوءٍ أَوْ مَكْرُوهٍ أَوْ خَدِيعَةٍ فَاحْرِقْ صَدْرَهُ وَحُطَّ مَكْرَهُ، وَارْدُدْ كَيْدَهُ فِي نَحْرِهِ، إِنَّكَ عَلَى كُلِّ شَيْءٍ قَدِيرٌ. وَصَلِّ اللّهُمَّ عَلَى سَيِّدِنَا مُحَمَّدٍ النَّبِيِّ الأُمِّيِّ وَعَلَى آلِهِ وَصَحْبِهِ وَسَلِّمْ.

53

TRANSLITERATION CODE

Arabic Letter	English Equivalent	Arabic Letter	English Equivalent
ث	th	ص	S
ج	j	ض	D
ح	H	ط	T
خ	kh	ظ	Z
ذ	zh	ع	accent before a vowel: 'a, 'i, 'o
ز	z	غ	gh
		ق	q

In transliterations, Arabic vowels are transcribed as follows:

a: for short 'alif' or standard 'a' (fut-Ha vowel), as in 'fatty', (rafa'a)

aa: for a long 'a' vowel, as in 'ran', 'man', (raami)

u: for a short 'a' vowel, as in 'but', 'what', (Subr)

o: for the 'o' vowel, as in 'today', 'pull', (mod)

oo: for long 'o' vowel, as in 'spoon', (laimoon)

i: for the 'i' vowel, as in 'win', 'sit', (min)

ee: for a long 'ee' vowel, as in 'teen', 'clean', (Teen)

Abbreviations:

(Bbuh) = Blessings be upon him

(RA) - raDiya Allahu 'anhu (or 'anha or 'anhum) Allah is pleased with him (or them)

BOOKS BY SAYYID DR AL-SHARIF ALHUSAINI NAQSHABANDI MUJADDIDI

1. The Compendium of Jewels: on your way to the Divine
2. The English Muslim's Companion
3. The Naqshabandi Supplications
4. The Madani Divine Openings in Salawat upon the Best of Creation (Peace and blessings be upon him)

All available on Amazon and blog: puresunnah.blogspot.com

Old holy Makkah